Soul Scapes

Pradhyuman

BookLeaf
Publishing

India | USA | UK

Acknowledgement

As I bring *Soul Scapes* to life, I want to take a moment to express my heartfelt gratitude to those who have supported me on this journey.

To my family, your unwavering love and encouragement have been my foundation. You have believed in me, even when I struggled to believe in myself. Thank you for your patience, understanding, and for providing a safe space where my creativity could thrive. Your faith in my voice has been a constant source of strength and inspiration.

To my friends, thank you for being my sounding board and my greatest cheerleaders. Your insights and feedback have enriched my work in ways I cannot fully express. Every conversation, every shared moment of laughter or contemplation, has shaped these poems and deepened my understanding of self-discovery.

I am also indebted to the poets and writers who have come before me, paving the way for those of us who seek to express our truths through words. Your work has urged me to look inward, to dig deeper, and to share my journey with authenticity.

And to you— whoever holds this book in your hands—thank you for allowing my words to find a home in your heart. It is my hope that these poems resonate with you, that they offer comfort, understanding, or simply a moment of reflection as you explore your own *soul scape.*

With all my love and appreciation,

— Pradhyuman

Preface

In the quiet moments of life—when the world slows, the noise fades, and solitude settles in—we often find ourselves face-to-face with the most profound questions: Who am I? What do I seek? What lies beneath the surface of my existence?

This collection of poems, *Soul Scapes*, is an exploration of those very questions—a journey into the heart of self-discovery.

Each poem is a step along a winding path, reflecting the vast spectrum of emotions and experiences that shape our identities. From moments of joy and clarity to those of doubt and introspection, these verses capture the essence of seeking oneself amidst the ever-shifting landscapes of life. They invite you to pause, breathe, and delve into the depths of our souls, revealing the beauty and complexity that resides within us all.

As you turn these pages, I encourage you to embrace your own journey. Allow the words to resonate with your experiences, stir memories, and spark new reflections. Poetry has the power to illuminate the hidden corners of our minds and hearts, and it is my hope that these poems serve as gentle guides along your path to self-awareness and understanding.

In sharing this collection, I hope to foster a sense of connection—between you, the reader, and the universal quest for meaning that binds us all. Let us embark on this journey together, navigating the landscapes of our souls and celebrating the unique stories that define who we are.

Welcome to *Soul Scapes*. May you find inspiration, solace, and perhaps a little piece of yourself within these pages.

— Pradhyuman

SEEKER

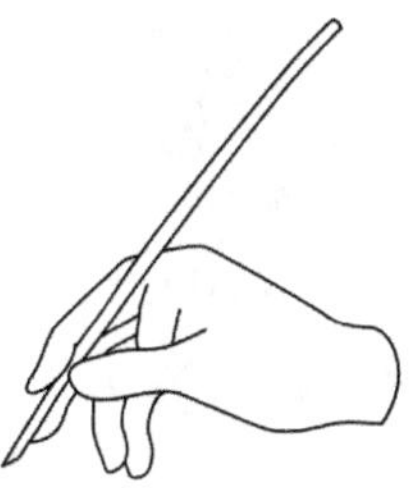

How do you seek your true self?
Is there path that leads you there?

What are the values that truly matter,
And how will you bring them to life?

What clarity do you need?
Is there a method that shapes who you are?

What routine will you set,
And how will you ensure you follow it?

How will you uncover these answers?
Have you asked yourself with absolute
honesty?

Journey

I like to spend time alone.
I like to wander far, on my own.

How far do I wish to go?
Where will this journey lead me?

Where did I once long to be,
And where have I arrived now?

Am I enjoying this journey,
Or have I lost myself along the way?

Do I know my self

Do I know myself clearly?
What is it that I seek from my life?

What passions do I long to pursue?
What activities ignite my soul?

Which places do I yearn to explore?
What food taste do I like the most?

Have I ever asked myself these questions?
Or am I living like machinery?

Roots of human suffering

What prevents me from being happy?
I couldn't find answer by myself.

As I read Patanjali Yoga Sutras,
It told me about Pancha Klesha.

Avidhya, Asmita, Raga, Dvesha,
Abhinivesha—
The very roots of human suffering.

How can I restore balance in my life?
I searched but found no answer within
myself.

As I read Patanjali Yoga Sutras,
It told me about Yamas and Niyamas.

Ahimsa, Satya, Asteya, Aparigraha,
Brahmacharya—
Will harmonize one's social interactions.

Saucha, Santosh, Tapah, Swadhyay, Ishwar
Pranidhana—
Will harmonize one's inner feelings.

Inner Core

A peaceful heart, a stable mind,
No desire at all.

Heart is calm, mind is steady,
There is no desire at all.

Emptiness prevails,
There are no thoughts at all.

Inner core alive,
There is no pain at all.

Inward Journey

An inward journey will not last too long
If you are not taking the Almighty along.

But will He walk this path with you?
Have you surrendered to Him or not?

How do I surrender myself?
Will He accept me or not?

His grace serves all,
He will not judge you along.

Building my life

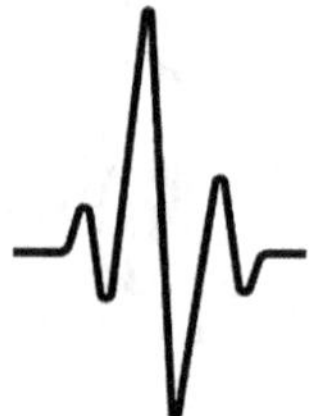

While I am finding myself,
I am also shaping my life.

Aligned in body, mind, heart, and spirit,
Let me break the boundaries of inner and
outer worlds.

Let me surrender to inner wisdom,
To guide myself through this journey.

Let me enjoy the adventure called life,
Without being bound by the weight of the
future.

Connect

How do I connect with myself
Before I connect with the world

Is it through examining
My thoughts, feelings and behavior

Is it through challenging
My own limitations and beliefs

Is it through experiencing
What is happening inside and outside of me

Or I need to lost myself
To connect with my true self

God

Does god exists in me ?
If yes, where does he resides

Is god in my heart?
That beats every second to make me realize

Is god in my mind?
Which connects me with everything

God resides in me
Yet seems far from reach

Din Chariya

How do I build a routine?
At what hour shall I rise?

What shall follow the break of dawn?
How shall I cleanse my body and soul?

How shall I nurture my body?
How shall I present myself to the world?

The concept of Dinchariya in Ayurveda
Offers me guidance along this path.

Shat karma

The body is a vessel to achieve everything,
How shall I cleanse and care for my body ?

How much should I eat?
What should I eat?

Mitahar, the yogic diet,
defines this balance with precision.

How shall I purify my being
To truly realize that I am alive?

Shatkarma, the sacred practice,
Guides me towards that realization.

Self-Realization

I seek peace and clarity,
How do I attain them?

From restlessness to stillness,
How do I make that journey?
To embrace stillness,
I must first dissolve Avidya.

Before I let it go,
Let me understand Avidya.

Avidya is false identification
With the body and mind.

Avidya can be transcended
 through self-realization.

Which path shall I walk
To uncover my true self?

Ashtanga Yoga is the way—
That leads to self-realization.

Chitta Prasadanam

We often get
Negative thoughts and feelings.

Default mechanism of mind
Breeds automatic negative thoughts.

Guilt, greed, envy, jealousy—
How do I transcend them?

Chitta Prasadanam must be cultivated
For stability of the mind.

Maitri towards Sukhi,
Karuna towards Dukhi.

Mudita towards virtuous,
Upeksha towards non-virtuous.

www.ingramcontent.com/pod-product-compliance
Lightning Source LLC
La Vergne TN
LVHW050849200726
843508LV00013B/2994